BOOK MARKETING TIPS FOR SELF-PUBLISHED AUTHORS

Lorraine M. Harris

DEDICATION

To my loving and supportive husband, Lamont and my daughters, Nicole and Natalie Harris Lenz and husband, Richard Scott Lenz. They are always supportive and encouraging.

ACKNOWLEDGEMENTS

No most difficult part of writing a book is editing it. No author can do it alone. I'm blessed to have a wonderful support group when it comes to helping me get to the final published book.

My continued source of keeping me grounded is my husband, Lamont and my daughters, Nicole and Natalie. Natalie is my biggest critic who give me the best, honest feedback.

I owe my talents and gifts. To keep me motivated, I rely on my favorite verse, Philippians 4:13, *"I know that I can do all things through him who strengthens me."*

The next individuals who critique what I write is my supportive writing group, The Write Corner. I can't thank Gloria (Gigi) Bagely-Lane enough for her friendship and taking the time to read and advise me on everything from the title to the content.

The last group of people I want to thank but can't name them all are the members of the Tampa Florida Writers Association. After conducting several workshops on marketing, they encouraged me to put my ideas in book form.

I take for responsibility for all mistakes and any liberties I might have taken.

INTRODUCTION

No words can describe the exhilaration, I felt holding my first book, *Sunday Golf.* I jumped up and down, cried and shouted. With tears running down my face, I exclaimed, "I can't believe it. My dream has come true."

Pausing, I cleared my throat. I clutched my book and murmured, "I hope someone reading my book, will like it.

My husband's facial expression concerned me. I waited for his reaction or words of support. Instead, he uttered, "You better hope someone buys it."

Confused, I asked, "What do you mean?"

With caution and in a soft voice, he explained. "Honey, I'm proud of your accomplishment, but no one knows who you are."

Regardless of his gentle manner, his words made me cringe. Rather than let the subject go. He continued. "Have you thought about your plan? You know, how are you going to sell your book?"

His questions swirled in my head. *A plan, sell what was he talking about?*

After several minutes, I answered him. "I'll do what other authors do. I'll have a book signing."

"That's great, but is that enough to sell your book on a continuing basis?" Before I could respond, Lamont hurried on.

"It's okay. You don't have to figure it out now, but you have to face reality. You have to do something to sell your book. It's not going to sell on its own."

I gave him a forced smile and said nothing. My shoulders relaxed, reminding myself that I wasn't alone in this publishing process. I had a publisher and they must do something other than publish my book. After all, they had invested in me.

After scanning my contract, I went numb. I, the author, had responsibility for marketing, promoting, and selling my book. The publisher would offer marketing services, but for a fee.

Being retired and on a fixed income, I didn't have the money to market my book. Rather than have a pity party, I made a list of my new responsibilities.

> ➤ Salesperson

- ➢ Book agent

- ➢ Publicist

- ➢ Promoter

- ➢ Website designer

- ➢ Presenter and probably much more

Making the list made the task of selling my book even more overwhelming. I took another approach and bought and borrowed books on the subject of marketing. I learned the following from those books.

- ➢ Information on the subject was massive.

- ➢ Much of the information didn't indicate what produced the best results.

- ➢ Most of the information spoke in generalities and didn't give the nuts and bolts of how to do it.

I'm not trying to paint a negative picture, but I felt ill-equipped. With all the books, I read there were three that I believe provided the most useful information.

- ➢ 1001 Ways to Market Your Books, John Kremer (Open Horizons 2009)

➢ Guerrilla Publicity, Jay Conrad Levinson, Rick Frishman, and Jill Lublin (Adams Media Corporation)

➢ How to Write, Print and Sell Your Book, Dan Poynter (ParaPublishing, 2009)

Disappointed and exhausted with my research, I took the next step. I talked to other published authors. After the discussions I felt discouraged. I learned nothing new. Below is what they shared.

➢ Have your publisher market, promote, and sell your book.

➢ Read books on the subject.

➢ Hire a publicist.

I knew my publisher's role. I read over 20 books on the subject and after looking into hiring a publicist, I couldn't afford one at $150 an hour, and that was a cheap quote.

Rather than continue researching, I made a list of who might buy my book.

➢ Relatives

➢ Friends

- ➢ Neighbors

- ➢ Friends of Friends

While I made my list, my husband glanced over my shoulder and said, "Your list looks good, but I doubt if everyone on that list is going to buy your book."

I groaned and rolled my eyes.

After contacting several family members and friends, Lamont was right. They were elated that I had written a book and expressed how proud they were and then asked, "When will I receive my autographed book?"

None of them said the word "free," but I understood what they meant. This made me think about people who buy books.

- ➢ People who are readers, but never buy books and brag about it. They borrow books from the libraries, friends, neighbors, and relatives.

- ➢ People that don't read but buy books to give for gifts on special occasions such as birthdays, anniversaries, and Christmas.

- ➢ People who read, but never buy new books. They buy their books at used book stores, flea markets, and yard sales.

➢ People who read, but no longer buy paper books because they own an electronic book.

➢ People who read a variety of books and buy them on a continuous basis. If they like an author, they talk about him or her and recommend others to buy their books.

After understanding who buys books, I realized that to capture people to buy my books, I had to market, promote, and sell my book. No one else was going to do it for me.

I picked certain strategies from the books I read and began implementing them. It didn't take long to understand that not all ideas worked. Some were more effective than others.

Marketing, promoting, and selling a book is a work-in-progress. I had to remind myself that my book wasn't written in a day, and the same applies to selling it.

Despite my reluctance to take on the task of selling my book, I began gaining exposure and success. By now, I had several published books and no longer had a publisher. I figured that if I had to market, promote, and sell my book, why have a publisher?

Not only that, other published authors started noticing my success and were curious. On a regular basis, authors asked, "What's your secret to selling your books?"

At first, I dismissed their question until I shared many of my ideas with authors and writing groups. I received positive feedback and they wanted to hear more of what I was doing.

Based on the authors reactions, I decided to write a book in a format that was easy to read, understand, and useful. Most of all the ideas I listed ideas that are:

➢ Effortless

➢ Cheap or free

➢ Time-saving

This book is not all-inclusive. Regardless how successful these ideas have worked for me, they may not work for other authors. Information was current at the time I wrote it.

Some of ideas may seem a little brazen while others probably aren't new or creative. That's okay. My goal is to give you a nudge and make you realize that you must market, promote, and sell your book.

Use your imaginative juices to sell your book. With time, I guarantee you'll come up with ideas that may be bolder than mine.

This book is a working document. Do the following for success.

- ➢ Do not try and implement everything at once.

- ➢ Take time to market, promote, and sell your book.

CHAPTER 1
MARKETING PLAN

You need a plan to market, promote, and sell your book. I learned the following about having a plan.

- ✓ It keeps you focused.

- ✓ It helps you to track your progress.

- ✓ It shows your progress.

My suggestion is to keep your plan simple. Think what you're going to do and how much time you're willing to spend on marketing, promoting, and selling your book.

Three easy ways to make your plan simple. Make three columns and include the following for tracking purposes.

- ✓ Strategies to implement.

- ✓ Date to implement the strategy.

- ✓ Track your progress.

CHAPTER 2
TEN WAYS TO BUILD A
CONTACT LIST

Once your book becomes published, you are overwhelmed when it comes to marketing your book. If you're like me, you'll say, "I don't know anyone who would buy my book."

To succeed, you need to build, maintain, and continue to add names to the contact list. Below are ideas to begin building a list.

1. **<u>PERSONAL ADDRESS BOOKS</u>**—Everyone has personal telephone and address books. Go through it and add to your contact list.

2. **<u>CHRISTMAS CARD LIST</u>**—Not everyone sends out Christmas cards but if you do, your list may be different than your personal address book.

3. **<u>HIGH SCHOOL YEARBOOK</u>**—If you have your high school yearbook, go through it and research to see if you can find addresses of your classmates.

4. **COLLEGE ALUMNI DIRECTORIES**—If you don't have a college alumni directory, obtain one. Go through it and add people's names to your contact list.

Helpful Contact List Tips:

➤ Go through your books and directories and make a list of the individuals' name, home and email addresses, and telephone number.

➤ Maintain your list on the computer or use a notebook binder.

Once you have your initial contact list started, you'll need to continue building it. Below are additional ways to do it.

5. **FAMILY REUNIONS**—There are lots of people that have family reunions. If your family has one, you might want to attend. You'll get to see relatives you know and meet ones you don't know.

Plan to the family reunion and do the following before you attend.

✓ Ask the host for family reunion coordinator if you can have a book signing. If the answer is no, take books with you. Once family members learn you're an author, they might want to buy one.

✓ Obtain names, email and home addresses, and telephone numbers.

✓ Keep track of anyone who buys your book and add them to your contact list.

✓ Pass out your business card.

6. **<u>CLASS REUNIONS</u>**—When you receive an invitation to attend your high school, college, or other type of school reunion. You should consider attending.

At the reunion, you will see old friends and introduce yourself to classmates you didn't know. Below are things you want to do before leaving the reunion.

✓ Ask the class reunion coordinator if you can have a book signing. If not, take books with you. Once your class mates learn you're an author, one of them might want to buy your book.

✓ Make sure you get a class reunion book that will have all your class mates' names, email and home addresses and telephone numbers.

✓ Keep track of who buys your book and add their name to your contact list.

7. **NEIGHBORHOOD DIRECTORIES**—Find out if your neighborhood has a directory of residents. Obtain one and listed below are some ideas you can do.

✓ Send postcards or invitations to your neighbors, telling them about your book.

✓ Have an author party, inviting less than ten neighbors. This will enable you the opportunity to talk about your book. Anyone who buys your book, make sure you add their name to your contact list.

8. **CHURCH**—If you attend church, sit in the same general area each time you attend. Introduce yourself to people and learn their names. After becoming familiar with a number of people, below are ideas you might do.

✓ Give out your business cards.

✓ Invite people to book signings.

✓ Ask if the church has a church directory and obtain it.

✓ Volunteer to be a guest speaker at special women programs or luncheons.

✓ Ask if the church has a book club. If so, volunteer to be a guest speaker to discuss your book.

✓ Keep track of anyone who buys your book and add their name to your contact list.

9. **ORGANIZATION/CLUB DIRECTORIES**—If you belong to an organization/club such as Rotary Club or Make sure you obtain the organization/club's directory. If you don't belong to an organization or club, ask a friend or neighbor if they will give you one of their directories.

✓ Send postcards or invitations to the organization or club members and invite them to a book signing.

Helpful Organization/Club Tip:

➢ Ask the person who gave you the organization or club directory if you can mention their name when sending out a postcard or invitation.

10. **EXCHANGE BUSINESS CARDS**—Do more than exchange or collect business cards. Obtaining business cards is an important way you can gather names, email and home addresses. When you receive a business card, you can do some of the following below items.

✓ Write on the back of business cards—who gave you the card; where you met the person, etc. Jot down anything that will help you remember the person.

✓ Review the collected business cards and determine if the individual can help you or maybe you can help the person.

✓ Send a letter to the person on the business card and tell them about your book.

Helpful Business Card Tip:

➢ When writing a letter to the name on the business card, say upfront how you met.

CHAPTER 3
CONTACT LIST FROM DIRECTORIES

You have a list started. Now comes the hard work. Finding ways to add names to the list. You can do that by gathering names of people you don't know from an array of directories. Below are examples of directories you can use.

NEIGHORHOOD DIRECTORY—Check to see if your neighborhood has a directory of the residents. If they have one, get it. Below is how you might use it.

- ✓ Increase your list by including the neighbor's home and email addresses.

Helpful Neighborhood Directory Tip:

- ✓ Create a neighborhood directory if one doesn't exist, explain the need for having it. You might say that it provides an opportunity for residents to know their neighbors and useful during emergencies.

CHURCH DIRECTORY—If you go to church, check to see if they have a membership directory, get a copy, and use it in several ways.

- ✓ Add church members' home and email addresses to your current contact list.

Helpful Church Directory Tips:

- ➢ When you attend church, sit in the same row or general area. Before the service begins, introduce yourself to people sitting near you and engage them in conversation. Weeks later and after you get to know the individuals, give the person a business card, get one from them and begin to build your own church directory.

- ➢ Depending on the size of the congregation, volunteer to make a church directory.

TELEPHONE DIRECTORY—Everyone receives a local telephone directory and you can use it in several ways.

- ✓ Start with the first name in the directory and add the name and home address.

ORGANIZATION/CLUB DIRCTORY—If you belong to an organization or club such as a Book Club, Rotary Club or Lion's Club, ask for a copy of the membership directory.

Helpful Organization/Club Directory Tips:

➢ If you don't belong to any organization or club, ask members for a copy of their membership directory. Tell the person why you want it and if you can use their name when sending out announcements regarding your book signing events.

➢ Be aware, you will spend money on the cost of paper or postcards, and stamps.

➢ Send a thank you note to the person who gave you a list of members.

FAMILY REUNION LIST—If your family has a family reunion, talk to the host for a copy of the relatives' home and email addresses.

CLASS REUNION DIRECTORY—When you attend a class reunion, make sure you receive a copy of the Class Reunion Directory. If one doesn't exist, ask the class reunion committee if you can have a copy of the list of class members' home and email addresses.

Helpful Tip:

➤ If a Class Reunion Directory doesn't exist, you might want to volunteer to make one for the next reunion.

CHAPTER 4
SOCIAL MEDIA CONTACT LIST

With technology, you might want to create a Social Media Contact List. If you aren't on social media, you may want to consider signing up to one of the sites.

FACEBOOK—If you have a Facebook account, this is a way to spread the word about your book.

TWITTER—Like Facebook, Twitter is another way to tell people about your book and add names to your contact list.

FACEBOOK FAN PAGE— Facebook is a free social media and social networking website. For authors, it's good to have a personal page as well as a Facebook Fan Page. Once you sign up you can use it to do a large number of activities.

- ✓ Create a profile.

- ✓ Upload photos.

- ✓ Upload videos.

✓ Send messages.

✓ Keep in touch with family, friends, authors and most importantly your readers.

This is an amazing way to promote yourself as an author; build awareness of who you are, and to advertise. Below are instructions for creating a Facebook Fan Page.

1. Sign up for Facebook. If you already have an account, log in.

2. Click on the settings, near the top right-hand corner of the page.

   ✓ Click on "Advertising."

   ✓ Look under Step 1: Build Your Facebook Page.

   ✓ Click on "Create a Page."

3. Click on the type of page you want to create. There are six categories—select "Artist" and author should appear.

4. Click on "Get Started."

5. Upload a profile picture.

6. Complete the About Section.

7. Decide whether you want to enable ads—this will cost and it can be expensive with little or no results.

Helpful Facebook Fan Page Tips:

➢ Creating the Fan Page can be tricky so view the tutorial.

➢ Go to www.facebook.com/page/guidelines.php where guidelines are available.

➢ Post often, authors need to keep their page current.

➢ Post pictures of all author events, not only book activities. Other pictures let readers know more about authors. For example, you ran in the Relay for Life 5K to raise money for cancer.

CHAPTER 5
TWENTY WAYS TO GAIN PUBLICITY

With little effort, authors can obtain publicity. It is a matter knowing where to get it and, in most cases, it's either cheap or free. Publicity is more about asking and being persistence.

1. **REQUEST MEDIA INTERVIEWS**—Obtaining media interviews will cost nothing. However, you do have to identify the media and ask for an interview. If you don't get the interview the first time, ask again.

   Most cities, towns and some communities have newspapers or newsletters. Contact the following media and ask for an interview.

   Newspapers:

   ✓ Identify local newspapers in your area.

   ✓ Identify newspapers outside your local area.

✓ Identify Internet websites that are interviewing authors.

Magazines:

✓ Identify local magazines in your area.

✓ Identify magazines outside of the local area.

Radio Stations:

✓ Identify local radio stations in your area.

✓ Identify radio stations outside your area.

✓ Identify Internet radio stations that may interview authors.

Television Stations:

✓ Identify local and cable television stations.

✓ Identify televisions outside your local area.

Helpful Publicity Tips:

➢ Send your book to the interviewer.

➢ Know your book's content, reread the book and take notes so you can answer questions about it.

➢ Make up interview questions, give them to the interviewer, and rehearse your answers.

➢ Provide your website during the interview.

➢ Provide details of any upcoming book signing.

➢ Make sure you tell where your book is sold.

➢ Try to schedule an interview before a book signing.

➢ Send a thank you note to the interviewer.

2. **GIVE BOOK REVIEWS**—It cost nothing for you to give a book review for another author. Your review might help the author sell books. Your review might gain you unexpected publicity and below are ways.

✓ Author may put your review in the Acknowledgement section of his or her book and mention that you're an author.

✓ Author may put your review on his or her website.

✓ People reading the book may see that you're an author and the person may want to learn more about you.

Helpful Review Tip:

➢ Provide the author with written permission to use your review.

3. **<u>PUBLISH ARTICLES</u>**—You're an author, why not gain exposure by writing articles. Research places where you can volunteer to write a one-time article or a regular recurring submitter to newspapers or magazines.

Writing articles is an excellent way for people to sample your writing. You can gain name recognition. In your by-line, make sure you add your website address.

<u>Helpful Article Writing Tips:</u>

➢ Identify local and free community newspapers. Ask to speak to the editor-in-charge and provide a sample article.

➢ Volunteer to write for a club newsletter.

➢ Create your own newsletter.

➤ Write articles for another author's newsletter.

4. **INTERNET ARTICLES**—You can write and submit articles on the Internet. Sites will publish and distribute the articles. In most cases, articles must be submitted in Word, PDF, or PowerPoint. Below are two popular sites that accept articles.

   ✓ www.ezinearticles.com

   ✓ www.ideamarketers.com

5. **BOOK CLUB GUEST SPEAKER**—Book clubs exist in most cities, towns, and communities. Find a book club. Ask if you can be a guest speaker. Below are suggestions of what you might do.

   ✓ Identify the club's person-in-charge.

   ✓ Send an informational package that includes your bio, website address, and book information.

   ✓ Send a free copy of your book.

6. **JOIN A WRITING GROUP**—Since you have skills, why not share them? Join a writing/critique group. Listed below are a list of benefits.

   ✓ Improve your listening, critiquing, and writing skills.

✓ Network with other authors.

✓ Gain name recognition.

✓ Become recognized as an expert in certain areas.

✓ Advertise your services to other authors.

7. **SHARE YOUR WRITING SKILLS**—Consider sponsoring a small writing/critique group. You may want to limit your group to ten or less members. This is a win-win situation. Forming a group benefits each member by honing his or her writing, listening, critiquing, and speaking skills.

8. **FORM AN ALLIANCE WITH AUTHORS**—Form an alliance by identifying authors who will promote your work and you do the same. Listed below are benefits for forming an alliance.

   ✓ Participate in a book signing or other event and put other author's promotional materials on your table.

   ✓ Take an author's books and promotional materials when you travel.

   ✓ Recognize published authors when giving speeches, having a party, teaching a course, or recommend an author's book to a book club.

9. **<u>BECOME A GUEST SPEAKER</u>**—Find ways where you can become a guest speaker. Let people know that you are available to discuss a variety of topics such as writing a book, publishing, and marketing. Below is a list of potential speaking opportunities.

✓ Book Clubs

✓ Church Groups

✓ Conferences

✓ Schools

✓ Libraries

✓ Cruise Ships

Helpful Guest Speaker Tips:

➢ Practice giving your talk using a tape recorder.

➢ Join Toastmasters to hone your speaking skills.

> Remember not all speaking engagements are about selling your book. Guest speaking can gain name recognition, visibility, and improve presentation skills.

> Volunteer at libraries to give a speech, hold a seminar, or participate in the library's scheduled programs.

10. **<u>BOOKSTORE BOOK SIGNINGS</u>**—The most common author event is to participate in a book signing. Book signings at bookstores cost you nothing but your time. Identify bookstores and ask to have a book signing.

Helpful Bookstore Book Signing Tip:

> Contact independent bookstores such as those selling used books. They seem more receptive to self-published authors having a book signing.

Successful Book Signing Tips:
Book signings can be frustrating and discouraging because you can sit for hours and not sell one book. Below are some suggestions to help with having a more successful book signing.

> Send out postcards or invitations to your book signing.

- Send out an email blast.

- Schedule a newspaper or magazine interview.

- Have a contest.

- Ask bookstore manager if you can leave bookmarks for customers.

- Ask the bookstore manager if you can post your event in the window.

- Ask nearby businesses if you can post your event in their windows and leave bookmarks for customers.

- Post your event on you Website.

- Have a friend on the day of the event, pass out information about your book signing.

Helpful Book Signing Tips:

- Use a table cloth.

- Have balloons or some other object to draw attention to your table.

> Give out your business cards.

> Obtain home and email addresses from everyone buying your book.

> Have a drawing.

> Talk to everyone and give them a business card, book excerpt, or bookmark.

11. **<u>NONTRADITIONAL BOOK SIGNING</u>**—Bookstores are not the only place to have a book signing. Look at other venues. Think out-of-the box. Listed below are some nontraditional places to have a book signing.

✓ Restaurants

✓ Flea markets

✓ Fairs

✓ Beauty Shops

✓ Barber Shops

✓ Bowling Centers

✓ Hospitals

- ✓ Churches

- ✓ Boutiques

- ✓ Shopping Centers

12. **<u>VOLUNTEER AT AUTHOR EVENTS</u>**—An easy way to gain name recognition, network, and to meet people is to volunteer at author events. Identify author events and ask if they need volunteers. Places to consider are conferences and book festivals.

13. **<u>SUPPORT AUTHORS</u>**—Show your support to other authors and hopefully they will do the same for you. Below is a list of items you can do.

- ✓ Create a buzz at an author's book signing.

- ✓ Write reviews for an author.

- ✓ Volunteer to help an author if you have editing, publishing, or proofreading skills.

14. **<u>ENTICEMENTS</u>**—Entice people to buy your book by giving discounts.

- ✓ Give discounts at book event.

✓ Give a discount when a person buys more than one book.

✓ Provide discount coupons.

15. **FORM A PARTNERSHIP**—Depending on your book's genre, identify organizations, businesses, associations, etc. that may have an interest in your book. Forming a partnership may benefit you in the following manner.

✓ They may place a large order for your book.

✓ They may invite you to be a guest speaker.

✓ They may give you free advertisement.

16. **BUILD A BOOKSTORE RELATIONSHIP**— Identify independent bookstores that may stock and sell your book. Build a relationship with the bookstore owner, staff, and customers. Below are ways to build a relationship.

✓ Visit the bookstore often and talk to the owner and staff.

✓ Talk to the customers.

17. **DONATE TO CHARITIES**—Identify charity foundations, organizations, associations, etc. that you might want to support. Tell the organization you intend to donate a specific percentage of the proceeds from the sale of your book. Do the following when you give your donation.

✓ Take a picture and put it in the newspaper.

✓ Let people know that when they buy your book that a portion goes to charity and tell them which one.

18. **ACCEPT ALL FORMS OF PAYMENT**—No author wants to miss the opportunity to sell a book. You should be prepared to accept all forms of payment.

✓ Cash

✓ Check

✓ Credit card

19. **TRAVELING**—When you travel and stay in one place for several days, weeks, or months, contact people you know, local libraries, newspapers, radio stations, etc. Below are things you can do.

✓ Request a book signing.

✓ Request an interview.

20.**<u>BOOKMARKS</u>**—You can use bookmarks as a cheap way to promote your book. Listed below are places to leave your bookmarks.

✓ Libraries

✓ Bookstores

✓ Airports

✓ Hotels

✓ Medical offices

✓ Hospitals

✓ Cruise Ships

✓ Beauty Shops

✓ Barber Shops

CHAPTER 6
FIFTEEN NAME RECOGNITION IDEAS

First time authors have difficulty obtaining name recognition. Even if people can't put a face with a name, it's important for people to know who you are. One way to achieve name recognition is through business cards. Decide how you want to obtain business cards. Below are some suggestions.

- ✓ Buy business cards. One of the cheapest places to buy business cards is at Vistaprint—www.vistaprint.com.

- ✓ Make your business cards,

- ✓ Obtain free business cards if you're in the military at www.militarybenefits.com.

BUSINESS CARDS—Below is fifteen quick, cheap, and easy ways you can obtain name recognition and introduce yourself to people.

1. Give your business card to everyone you meet.

2. Put your business card on bulletin boards found in grocery stores, laundry mats, and restaurants.

3. Ask friends and relatives to give your business cards to people they know or meet.

4. Put a business card inside postage envelopes when renewing a magazine subscription.

5. Put a business card inside postage paid envelopes where someone is asking for a donation.

6. Put a business card inside postage paid envelopes when banks, magazines, etc. solicit.

7. Put a business card inside magazines that are in medical offices, barber and beauty shops, and nail shops.

8. Write on the back of your business card— "Here's the book I was telling you about." "A good read." "This book is awesome." "This book is worth reading." Then leave it.

9. Take a stroll and place a business card on outdoor dining tables, food court, airports, etc.

10. Leave a business card in hotel rooms.

11. Place your business card in restaurant bowls where there is a weekly drawing.

12. Put your business card with any cash donation you make.

13. Put your business card inside the restaurant menu.

14. Put your business card inside the payment holder when paying the restaurant bill.

15. Leave business card on cruise ships.

Helpful Tips:

➢ Carry your business card at all times.

➢ Carry paperclips. Use them to attach your business card to menus, cash donations, and magazines.

CHAPTER 7
TEN WAYS FOR PUBLICITY

Most people don't know who you are. You should do whatever it takes to market, promote, and sell your book. Below are ten ways to do just that.

GIVE YOUR BOOK AWAY—People like free things. Below are ten ways to gain name recognition, sell books, and gain publicity.

1. Give an autographed book to charity, clubs, and schools for door and raffle prizes.

2. Give books to local and out-of-state libraries.

3. Give books to private libraries such as retirement communities, nursing homes, churches, etc.

4. Give books to local and out-of-state prison libraries at www.prisonbookprogram.com.

5. Give a book to those serving in the military at www.booksforsoliders.com.

6. Give a book to cruise ship libraries. If you don't cruise but know those that do, ask them to take your book and put it in the cruise ship library.

7. Give a book to www.bookshare.org.

8. Give children books to private nursery schools.

9. Register a book, follow the instructions and give it away at www.bookcrossing.com.

10. Hold a contest and give away an autograph book on your website.

CHAPTER 8
MARKETING YOUR BOOK TEN WAYS

Marketing doesn't have to be time consuming or expensive. Marketing is ongoing and can be done any time and it doesn't matter when your book was published.

1. **SPONSOR A CONTEST**—At any time you can sponsor a contest. Be creative, think outside the box. Examples of contests are: name the book, name the main character, or name the town.

2. **ENTER CONTESTS**—Identify legitimate contests to enter. Many are listed in the yearly published Writer's Market Book. Do the following when entering contests.

✓ Determine the contest cost.

✓ Follow the rules and don't miss the deadline date.

Benefits of winning a contest.

- ✓ An author's work is validated.

- ✓ An author receives feedback from the judge about the work submitted. Many of the judges are published authors, agents, and publishers.

- ✓ Authors can use the title, "Award Winning Author."

3. **ADVERTISE**—Advertisement doesn't have to be expensive. Take advantage of the unusual places listed below for advertising.

- ✓ Church Bulletins.

- ✓ Funeral Home Bulletins.

- ✓ Organizations/club Newsletters.

- ✓ Partner with other authors to advertise to cut down on the cost.

4. **BOOK RELATED MERCHANDISE**— Create book related merchandise to advertise your book, gain exposure, and name recognition. Identify local places that make T-Shirts, mugs. caps, pencils, etc. or go on the Internet.

Below are Internet sites that makes the above-mentioned merchandise.

✓ CafePress—www.cafepress.com.

✓ VistaPrint—www.vistaprint.com

✓ Kleenex—www.kleenex.com

Helpful Merchandise Tip:

➤ Put your website address on everything you make.

5. **PRESS RELEASES**—Develop an eye-catching press release title that will make the reader want to read it. In the body of the release talk about your book. Press releases can increase media visibility; create a buzz; offer cheap advertisement; and generate website traffic.

Helpful Press Release Tips:

➤ Press releases are limited to one page.

➤ Research the Internet that accept press releases.

6. **HOME BOOK PARTY**—Sponsor a home book party event. The party will be similar to a

Tupperware or jewelry party. Decide where to have the party, perhaps a friend will have it for you. Decide who to invite and ask all guests to bring their address book with them. At the party, ask the guests if you can send ten of their friends a letter about your book.

Helpful Home Book Signing Tips:

➢ Show your guests the letter you intend to send their friends.

➢ Send your guests a thank you note.

7. **<u>BOOK REVIEWS</u>**—Ask authors to read your book and write a review. Ask people who bought your book for a review. Below are rewards from receiving book reviews.

✓ Reviews let you and others know what they think about your book.

✓ Reviews serve as testimonies.

✓ Reviews validate your work.

✓ Reviews can help sell your book.

Helpful Book Review Tips:

➢ Post reviews on your website and other Internet sites.

➢ Place reviews on the back cover or inside of your book, as appropriate.

8. **ADDRESS RETURN LABELS**—Advertise by creating return address labels that you make or buy. Put a picture of your book and website address on the label.

✓ Place return labels on outgoing mail.

✓ Put return labels on anything requesting an address label.

9. **DONATE MAGAZINES**—Donate used magazines to medical offices, beauty and barber shops, nail shops, etc. Below is what you might do before leaving the magazines.

✓ Replace subscription mailing address label with your author return label.

10. **INTERNET INTERVIEWS**—Use all means for requesting an interview—Internet, newspaper, magazine, radio and TV interviews.

CHAPTER 9
WAYS TO GAIN INTERNET PRESENCE

You need to use the Internet to its fullest and you don't have to spend a lot of time doing it. Start slow and build a presence, using 5-10 minutes a day or 30-60 minutes a week. In today's world of technology, you should make use of what is available on the Internet.

Authors often wonder if they need a website. It's a necessity to have one. Below are some reasons why an author must have a website.

- ✓ Build credibility.

- ✓ Sell your book, 24-7.

- ✓ Create a network of supporters, fans, and readers.

- ✓ Promote your events and signings.

- ✓ Make yourself available to the media.

- ✓ Sell book related merchandise.

WEBSITES—Hire a professional to create your website, ask another author, or do it yourself. To create a website and your inexperience, use one of the free websites mentioned below and practice.

- ✓ www.freewebs.com

- ✓ www.wix.com

- ✓ www.weebly.com

ADVERTISE USING EMAIL ADDRESS—Create an email signature using your email address. Once you add your website to your email address signature, it will automatically appear.

PROMOTE EVENTS—When you're going to host or participate in an event, post it on the following free websites.

- ✓ www.authorsandexperts.com--Authors and Experts

- ✓ www.upcoming.org--Upcoming Events

- ✓ www.authorsden.com--Authorsden

EARN MONEY EFFORTLESSLY—Authors can make money by doing nothing more than creating an account with one of the websites listed below. You earn money every time a person visits your website and clicks on the link to the website. The amount of money earned isn't a lot, but it's worth signing up. Listed below are the most popular affiliate websites.

- ✓ www.amazon.com

- ✓ www.barnesandnoble.com

- ✓ www.linkshare.com

- ✓ www.clickexchange.com

LOCATE BOOK EVENTS—Below are websites where you can find information about book events.

- ✓ www.loc.gov/loc/cfbook/bookkkfair

- ✓ www.booksigningusa.net

- ✓ www.bookfairs.com

INTERNET BOOK SELLING—Although your book is selling on Internet sites such as Amazon and Barnes and Noble, there are other sites where you can sell your book.

- ✓ www.ebay.com

- ✓ www.lulupress.com

✓ www.Craigslist.com

BLOGS—Create a blog and write tips, articles, etc. You can provide information about your book and anything else you want to share with your readers or other authors. Create an account and start.

✓ www.blogger.com

✓ www.typepad.com

✓ www.wordpress.com

CREATE LINKS—Create a link from your website to other author related sites and blogs. Ask authors if you can link your site to theirs and vice versa.

WHERE ARE YOUR BOOKS SELLING—Most books are sold on Amazon and Barnes and Noble, but there are other Internet sites selling your book. Below are sites where you can see other places that sell your books.

✓ www.bestbookdeal.com

✓ www.bookmarket.ning.com

✓ www.fetchbook.com

JOIN RELEVANT WEBSITES—You should identify relevant websites that provide opportunities to market, promote and sell your book. These sites require you to sign up and no other action.

- ✓ www.jacketflap.com

- ✓ www.redroom.com

- ✓ www.authornation.com

BOOK CLUB DISCUSSION—You should have a page dedicated to book clubs in case your book is selected for their members to read. You should develop questions that the book club can use during their meetings.

Helpful Book Club Discussion Tips:

- ➢ Write at least 5-10 questions.

- ➢ Provide open ended questions that will generate a discussion.

FACEBOOK/TWITTER—If you have a Facebook or Twitter account, this is an ideal place to spread the word about your book. You can gather email addresses to add to your contact list.

LEND YOUR EXPERTISE—Become an author who is willing to answer writing related questions. If you can spend a few minutes a week on the sites listed below you'll soon become known as an expert with answers.

- ✓ www.answers.yahoo.com

- ✓ www.askme.com

SEARCH ENGINES—After having an Internet presence, you need to drive traffic to your website. Below are two search engine sites.

- ✓ www.addme.com--a site with a host of free services to help drive traffic to your website.

- ✓ www.submit-it.com--a fee-based site with elaborate packages for driving traffic to your website.

BANKING ONLINE—PayPal is an online financial bank. By signing up for PayPal and placing their button on your website, it's an easy way for your readers to buy your book.

CHAPTER 10
TEN WAYS TO USE AMAZON

Amazon is not just a place to sell books. Amazon has an abundance of opportunities for authors to market, promote, and sell books. You can use it as a place to establish an author's presence.

1. **REQUEST READERS FOR REVEWS**—You should ask and encourage anyone who read your book to write a review. Explain to relatives, friends, and supporters how reviews help sells your book.

   Helpful Reader Review Tip:

   ➢ Provide your book to authors and ask them to write a review for your book.

2. **AUTHORS WRITE REVIEWS**—You should get into a habit of writing book reviews on Amazon. Any time you read a book, write a review and post it.

3. **AUTHORS PAGE**—Amazon's Author Page is for published authors to provide readers with information about you. You can promote yourself and gain name recognition.

4. **ADVANTAGE PROGRAM**—You can sign up on Amazon's Advantage Program and sell your book.

5. **READERS LOOK INSIDE YOUR BOOK**—A way that Amazon entices readers to buy your book is to let them read several chapters.

6. **EARN MONEY ON AMAZON**—Join Amazon's affiliate program and make money advertising Amazon's products on your website. People follow the link and you earn up to 15% if the person buys the product.

7. **AMAZON'S PROFILE PAGE**—When you set up your profile, include "author" after your name. Every time you write a review or make a comment on a product, your name along with author appears. For example, it will read, John Smith, Author.

8. **LINK WEBSITES TO AMAZON**—You can provide a link from your book to Amazon. When a person clicks on the book, it will lead them to Amazon where they can buy your book.

9. **<u>PUBLISH BOOKS USING AMAZON</u>**— Through Amazon's CreateSpace, authors can have books published.

10. **<u>AMAZON'S KINDLE BOOK</u>**—After your book is published through CreateSpace, you can upload your files and have it become an electronic book for Kindle.

CHAPTER 11
TEN WAYS TO GAIN VISIBILITY

On a regular basis, you need to think of ways to attain visibility. Photos enhance an author's credibility by showing what they're doing.

VISIBILITY—Being visible is easier than most authors think. Below are some easy ways to obtain visibility.

1. Take pictures at author events.

2. Take pictures of other authors participating in different activities such as MS Walk, Cancer Golf Tournaments, etc.

3. Post pictures on photo sharing sites. People will have a change to see what you're doing.

   ✓ www.flickr.com

   ✓ www.photobucket.com

   ✓ www.shutterfly.com

4. Participate in your favorite activity to meet and network with people.

5. Learn a new activity to meet and network with people.

6. Accept offers from people wanting to take your picture.

7. Accept interview offers from newspapers, magazines, and bloggers.

8. Volunteer for author and non-related author activities. It gives you a chance to meet and network people.

9. Take pictures when out-of-town, on vacations, etc.

10. Take pictures everywhere and anywhere.

Helpful Visibility Tips:

➤ Carry a camera even though you can take pictures with your cell phone.

➤ Post your pictures on social media, Facebook, Twitter, and Instagram.

➤ Post pictures on your website.

➢ Ask authors if they have any pictures they might have taken at an event and ask for a copy of the picture.

CHAPTER 12
TEN WAYS TO PUBLICIZIE EVENTS

Authors need help trying to encourage people to attend their events. Try to find ways to promote an event.

POST EVENTS—One of the easiest ways to promote book signings, workshops, and other events, is to post them on various websites.

1. www.booktours.com

2. www.authorsandexperts.com

3. www.upcoming.org

4. www.eventful.com

5. www.craiglist.com

6. Post events on your website.

7. Ask others to post your event.

8. Use websites where you're a member to post events.

9. Take out a newspaper ad.

10. Advertise in a magazine.

CHAPTER 13
TEN WAYS TO USE WEBSITE ADDRESS

Okay, you don't have time to market, promote, and sell your book. There are ways you can do it by using the Internet. You must have a website to do the following ten ideas. Put your website address (URL) as suggested.

1. Put on the back of your book.

2. Put on the inside your book.

3. Place on your business card.

4. Add to your email address.

5. Add on handout material.

6. Add on bookmarks.

7. Write a check and add it.

8. Add to your voicemail

9. Write notes and add it after your signature.

10. Send a greeting card and add it after your signature.

CHAPTER 14
EIGHT WAYS TO VALIDATE AN AUTHOR'S WORK

No matter if you're self-published a traditional author, everyone likes to have their work validated. Endorsement of an author's work can boost one's confidence and help sell books.

VALIDATION OF AUTHOR'S WORK—Below are ten ways you can have your book validated.

1. Ask readers for a review.

2. Ask a famous or local celebrity for a review.

3. Post unsolicited comments and testimonies left on your website.

4. Ask authors for a review.

5. Write a book related to medicine, child safety, etc. and ask a professional in the field for a review.

6. Write a book on a particular organization, business, etc. and ask for a review.

7. Win a contest and become an "Award Winning Author."

8. Obtain reviews from professional reviewers.

Helpful Validation Tips:

➤ Post reviews on your website and other appropriate websites.

➤ Ask readers to post their review on appropriate websites selling your book such as Amazon, Barnes and Noble, etc.

➤ Put the review on the back of your book.

➤ Put the review on the inside of your book.

➤ Ask authors to put their review on their website.

➤ Mention your award-winning status on your bio, websites, and in book.

➤ Ask for permission to use a review.

CHAPTER 15
ASK FOR HELP

Selling your book is a business. Most successful entrepreneurs aren't afraid to ask for help and neither should authors. Below are ten opportunities for authors to ask relatives, friends, and neighbors to help with your book.

1. Ask relatives, friends, and neighbors to buy your book.

2. Help relatives, friends, and neighbors write a review of your book.

3. Tell relatives, friends, and neighbors that you're available to speak at events such as book clubs, libraries, and churches.

4. Ask relatives, friends, and neighbors to loan your book to their friends.

5. Ask relatives, friends, and neighbors to donate your book to public and private libraries

6. Give your business card to your relatives, friends, and neighbors to give to people.

7. Ask relatives, friends, and neighbors to visit libraries and ask them about your book.

8. Make sure your relatives, friends, and neighbors know where your book is sold.

9. Give relatives, friends, and neighbors your promotional materials that they can to people or to leave at appropriate places.

10. Ask relatives, friends, and neighbors if they have any skills that might help you such as editing, website design, and marketing.

Helpful Tips:

➤ Give relatives, friends, and neighbors a free book if you want them to help you.

➤ Acknowledge relatives, friends, and relatives for their help.

CHAPTER 16
HELP OTHER AUTHORS

You can support other authors regardless if they do the same. Below are fifteen ways to help fellow authors.

1. Tell people that your friend is an author.

2. Encourage people to buy you're the author's book.

3. Recommend the author's book to a book club.

4. Suggest that people visit the author's website for information of him or her.

5. Ask the author for business cards and give them to people you know and meet.

6. Write a review of the author's book and post it on your website and other websites where the book is sold.

7. Write a review or testimonial that the author can use in the book's introduction or on the back of the book.

8. Host a book signing for the author.

9. Give the author's book away as a gift for special occasions such as birthday, Christmas, or Mother's Day.

10. Set up a link from your website to the author's website.

11. Acknowledge an author who may be attending one of your events. As appropriate, give the author several minutes to talk his or her book.

12. Recommend an author to be a guest speaker.

13. Post an author's events.

14. Offer your skills to an author.

15. Interview an author for your website, newsletter, or blog.

CHAPTER 17
TRAVELING

Traveling is an opportunity for you to market, promote, and sell your book. Below are some things to do while traveling.

1. **Libraries**—put your book in out-of-state libraries.

2. **Interviews**—ask for newspaper, radio and TV station interviews.

3. **Cruise Ships**—put your book in the cruise ship library.

4. **Hotels**—leave a book or promotional materials in the hotel drawer.

5. **Airplane**—leave a book or promotional materials in the airplane seat pockets.

6. **Book Signing**—ask to have a book signing before you visit a city.

7. **Guest Speaker**—identify organizations where you can be a guest speaker.

8. **<u>Business Cards</u>**—give them to people you meet and leave them at places you visit.

CHAPTER 18
CONTINUE SELLING YOUR BOOK

After the buzz of your newly published book dies down, how will you continue to sell your book? Remember marketing is a continual process. Below are ways an author can continue selling his or her book.

1. **Business cards**—On a daily basis, discover ways to give your business card away or to leave it somewhere.

2. **Website**—Update your website on a regular basis. Create ways for people to visit your website such as giving away a newsletter, having contests, and giving updates on what you're working on.

3. **Blog**—Create a blog if you don't have one and update it by posting new blogs at least once a month. Do things such as interviewing authors, writing articles on writing, and linking your blog to other blogs and websites.

4. **Track Progress**—You should keep track of what book selling strategies work. Decide on what you'll continue doing what ones to discontinue.

5. **Author Friendly Websites**—If you signed up for websites such as AuthorsDen, Goodreads, and Amazon's Author Page, you should visit them at least once a month to update your information.

6. **New Strategies**—You should look for new ways to market, promote, and sell your book.

   Helpful New Strategy Tips:

   ➢ Listen to what other authors are doing to market, promote, and sell their books.

   ➢ Consider marketing ideas not specific to selling books and use.

   ➢ Consider how to modify what you're doing and put a different twist to the strategy.

7. **Guest Speaker**—You should continue seeking ways to become a guest speaker. Below are organizations that are always looking for speakers.

   ✓ Book Clubs

   ✓ Libraries

✓ Cruise Ships

✓ Rotary Clubs

✓ Churches

8. **Press Releases**—You should send out press releases at least once a month. Find new angles when writing a press release. Make the press release eye-catching. Write the press release heading less about your book and more about what will grab the reader's attention.

9. **Internet Presence**—Continue to find author friendly websites that give you a chance to promote your book.

Helpful Internet Presence Tips:

➢ Make sure it's easy to sign-up to the websites.

➢ Check the cost of the website.

➢ Understand the website's requirement.

10. **Social Media**—Sign-up for social media websites and post often for visibility and name recognition.

11. **Ask for Help**—Continue to ask people for help.

12.**Contests**—Continue to research places that sponsor legitimate contests and enter.

CHAPTER 19
SUCESSFUL MARKETING TIPS

Authors have no choice but to market, promote, and sell their books. While doing so, remember you are in control.

Ten ways to have success with your book.

1. **Plan**—decide what strategies you want to use when marketing, promoting, and selling your book.

2. **Positive**—be passionate when selling your book.

3. **Proactive**—take the time to market, promote, and sell your book.

4. **Prioritize**—decide which strategies to carry out and stick to them.

5. **Prepare**—sell your book at every opportunity.

6. **Persistence**—don't give up because you aren't seeing the results of your hard work right away.

7. **Praise**—give thanks to everyone who helps you.

8. **Pause**—take time to reflect on your goals and how you're going to achieve them.

9. **Patience**—it takes time to see results.

10. **Power**—you have power, now use it.

RESOURCES

Authors need to research before marketing, promoting, and selling their books. In doing so, an author can find many helpful books on the topic. It can overwhelm you but don't let it stop you from marketing, promoting, and selling your books.

As mentioned before, I found the following books the most helpful.

- ➤ 1001 Ways to Market Your Books, John Kremer (Open Horizons 2009)

- ➤ Guerrilla Publicity, Jay Conrad Levinson, Rick Frishman, and Jill Lublin (Adams Media Corporation)

- ➤ How to Write, Print and Sell Your Book, Dan Poynter (ParaPublishing, 2009)

ABOUT THE AUTHOR

Lorraine M. Harris is a native of Connellsville, Pennsylvania. She retired from the United States government after 34 years. She and her husband, Lamont moved from the Washington, D.C. metropolitan area to The Villages, Florida. They have two daughters, Nicole and Natalie, and a son-in-law, Scott.

As an award-winning author, she conducts workshops and seminars, and teaches courses. She speaks at libraries, book clubs, writing groups and high schools.

Lorraine is a lifetime member of the Florida Writers Association, founder of the Write Corner and member of The Writers League of the Villages.

Since retiring to The Villages, she authored and published numerous fictional books. She has won the National Novel Writing Month (NaNoWriMo) award for three years. In 2008, Lorraine received the honor of Author of the Year by the Artists of America (AOA) in California. AOA provides children in the inner city with opportunities to learn about the arts. In 2011, the African American Golfers Board inducted her in the African American Hall of Fame as the "2011 Golf Publisher of the Year."

Lorraine lives by the saying, *"We make a living by what we get, and we make a life by what we give."* She donates portions of her book sales to a variety of charities.

BOOKS BY LORRAINE

SUNDAY GOLF
AFTER BOWLING
GOLF COURSE VIEW
CASSEROLE PARADE
CASSEROLES, LOVE & SURPRISES
NOT THE NORM, A SMALLTOWN STORY
IT COULD HAPPEN TO YOUR CHILD
BEHIND CLOSED DOORS
LIVING WITH DECEPTION
REGAL CARE, SENIOR LUXURY LIVING
SURVIVING THE LIE
AMY'S ADVENTUROUS BUS TRIP
AMY'S AUTUMN SPLENDOR
INTUITION, CO-AUTHOR, DEBORAH SEIBERT

SELF-HELP BOOKS

MAH JONGG FOR SENIORS, GUARANTEED
SENSIBLE, SUCCESSFUL BOOK MARKETING
TIPS

To obtain additional information about the author, visit her website, www.lorrainemharris. All Lorraine's books are available on Amazon, Barnes and Noble, and other Internet sites selling books.

A NOTE FROM LORRAINE

Thank you for reading, *"Book Marketing Tips for Self-Published Authors."* If you found the book helpful, I would love to hear from you.

Please take the time and leave a short review on my website, Amazon.com, Twitter, Instagram, or Facebook. Reader reviews help new readers make decisions about buying my book.

I value and appreciate each and every reader who buys my book. Thank you for your support.

Please tell your friends. Word of mouth is my best friend and the single most effective way for selling my books.